T0402929

INTRO TO CHEMISTRY | Need to Know

# The Periodic Table

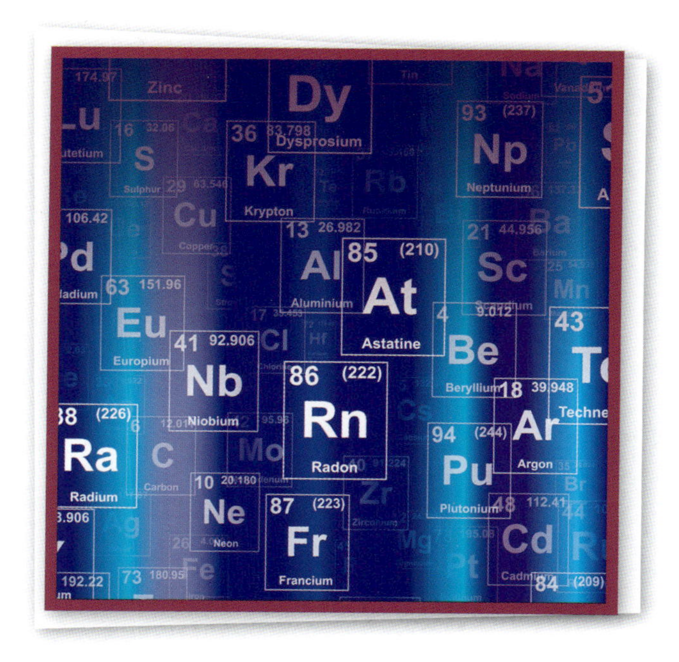


by Daniel R. Faust

Consultant: Sara Vogt
Science Educator at Anoka Hennepin School District

Minneapolis, Minnesota

**Credits**
Cover and title page, © Eyematrix/iStock; 5, © michaeljung/Shutterstock; 7, © suksan yodyiam/Shutterstock; 14, © Dewin ID/Shutterstock; 21, © Parilov/Shutterstock; 23, © Bjoern Wylezich/Shutterstock; 25, © SPCOLLECTION/Alamy; and 27, © D-VISIONS/Shutterstock.

**Bearport Publishing Company Product Development Team**
President: Jen Jenson; Director of Product Development: Spencer Brinker; Senior Editor: Allison Juda; Editor: Charly Haley; Associate Editor: Naomi Reich; Senior Designer: Colin O'Dea; Associate Designer: Elena Klinkner; Associate Designer: Kayla Eggert; Product Development Assistant: Anita Stasson

*Library of Congress Cataloging-in-Publication Data*

Names: Faust, Daniel R., author.
Title: The periodic table / by Daniel R. Faust.
Description: Minneapolis, Minnesota : Bearport Publishing Company, [2023] | Series: Intro to chemistry: need to know | Includes bibliographical references and index.
Identifiers: LCCN 2022033678 (print) | LCCN 2022033679 (ebook) | ISBN 9798885094276 (library binding) | ISBN 9798885095495 (paperback) | ISBN 9798885096645 (ebook)
Subjects: LCSH: Chemical elements–Juvenile literature. | Periodic table of the elements–Juvenile literature.
Classification: LCC QD467 .F38 2023 (print) | LCC QD467 (ebook) | DDC 546/.8–dc23/eng/20220713
LC record available at https://lccn.loc.gov/2022033678
LC ebook record available at https://lccn.loc.gov/2022033679



For more information, write to Bearport Publishing, 5357 Penn Avenue South, Minneapolis, MN 55419.

# Contents

# Finding What You Need

A library is full of books. But with thousands of titles, how do you find the one you want? The library is organized to make it easier.

Scientists who study chemicals have to do the same thing. They organize all the **elements**. They put them on the periodic table.

At libraries, books are shelved based on subject. Then, they are often further divided by title or author name. The elements in the periodic table are also organized in multiple ways.

# A Chemical Library

Elements are all around you. They are the basic things that make up everything in this world and beyond. The periodic table lists all the known elements. It's easy to find elements on the table if you know what you're looking for.

Oxygen is an element in the air all around us. We need to breathe it to stay alive. Graphite (GRAF-ite) in pencils allows us to write.

Graphite is a form of the element carbon.

# Looking Inside

To understand the periodic table, first we need to look inside elements. Each element is made of **atoms**. These very small parts are broken into even smaller parts. **Protons** and **neutrons** are found in a nucleus. They stay at the center of each atom.

An element may be made of a single atom. Other times, elements are two or more of the same kind of atoms bonded together.

# A Model of an Atom

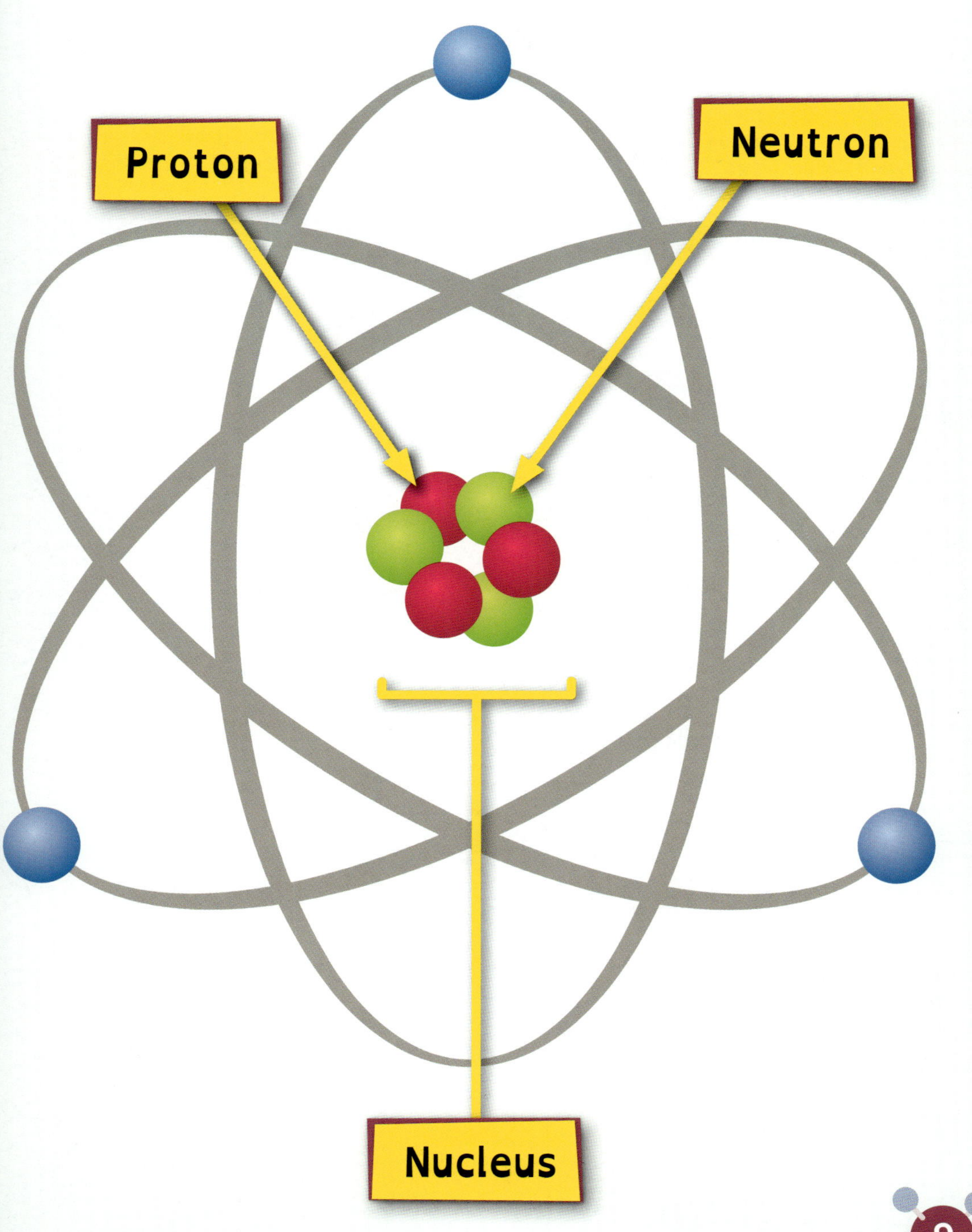

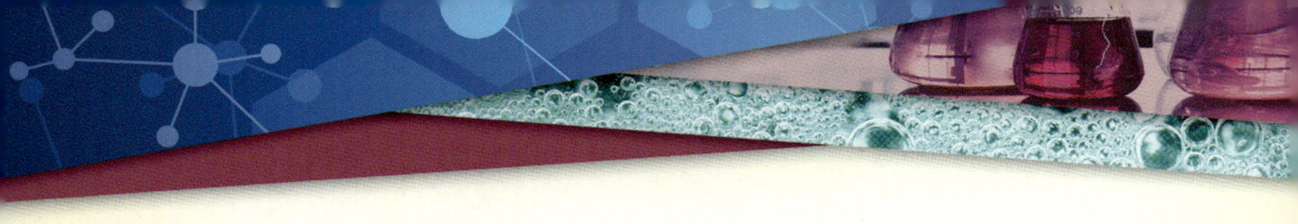

**Electrons** travel around the nucleus. They stay in paths called electron shells. Each atom can have many electron shells, but every shell can hold only so many electrons. There may be anywhere from 2 to 32 electrons in a shell. The number depends on the element and the specific shell.

All of the atoms of each element have the same number of electron shells. They often share a similar number of protons, neutrons, and electrons.

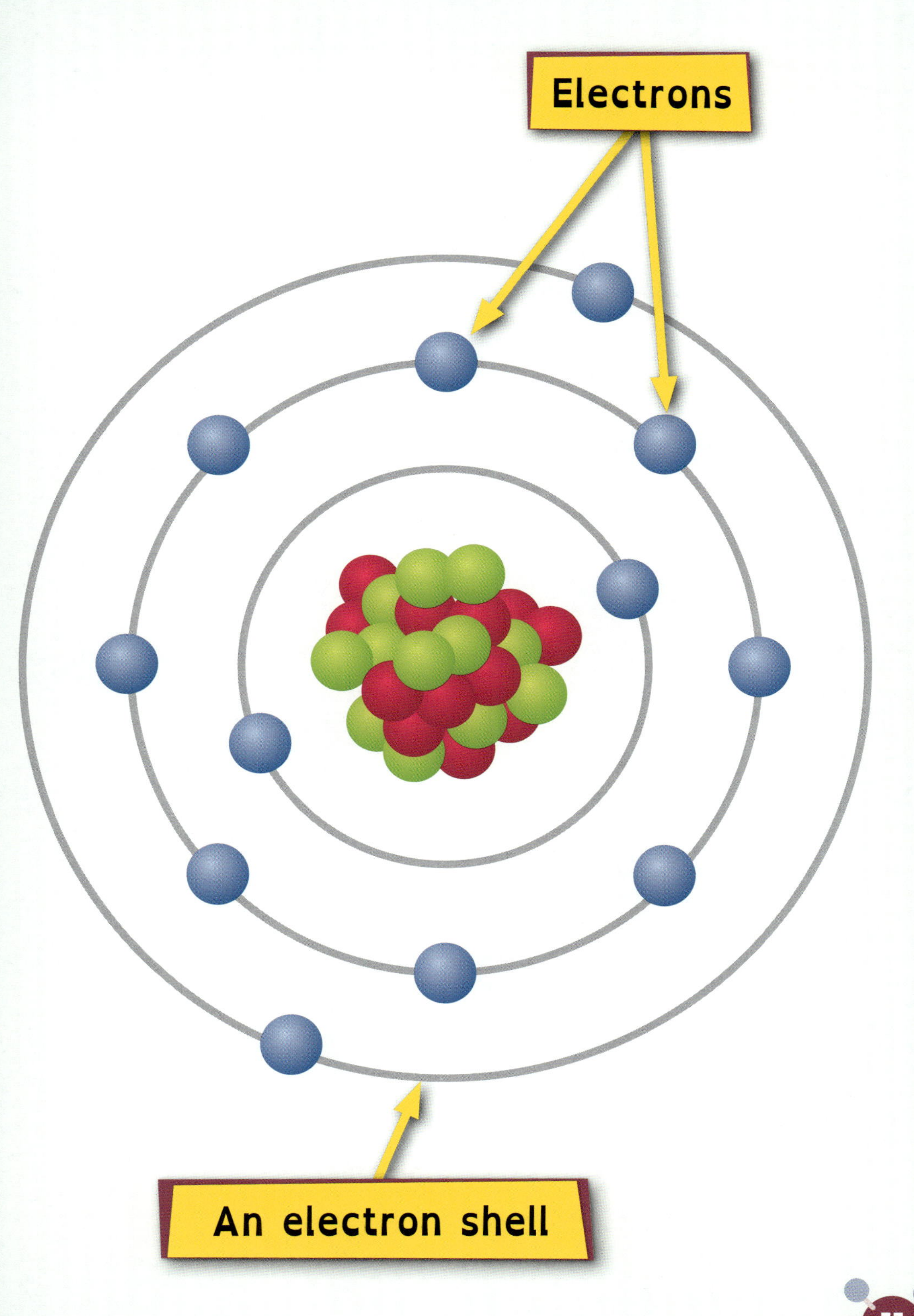
Electrons
An electron shell

# What's in the Box?

What do atoms have to do with the periodic table? Each element is placed in a box on the table based on its atoms. First, an element is given an atomic number. This number matches the number of protons in each atom of an element.

Right now, there are elements numbered 1 through 118. That means we know of elements that have anything from 1 to 118 protons.

# A Nitrogen Atom

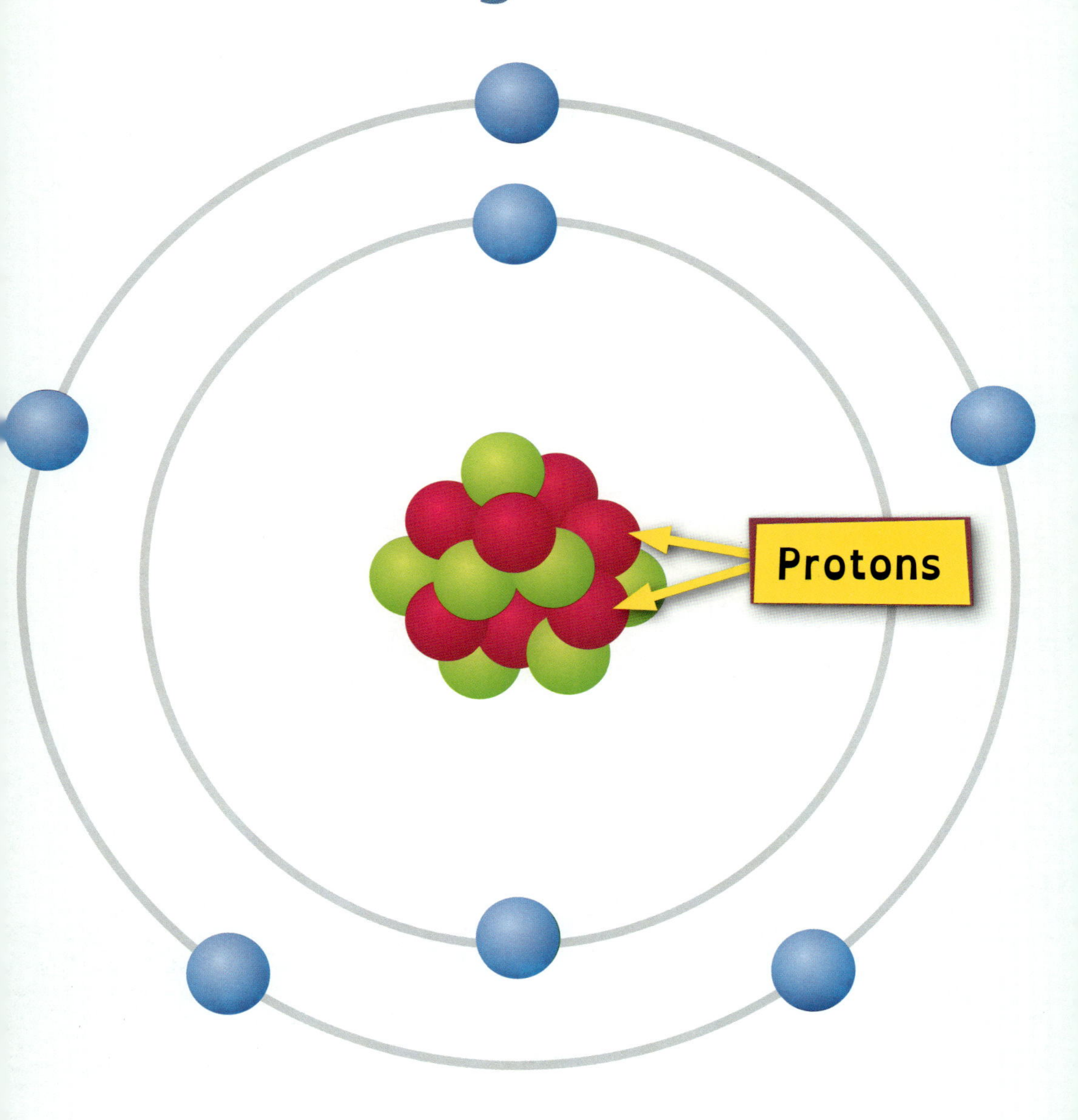


The element nitrogen's atomic number is 7. It has 7 protons.

Each element on the table has an atomic mass. This tells how many protons and neutrons scientists can expect in the average atom of the element.

The table also includes letters that stand for each element's name. This is its chemical symbol.

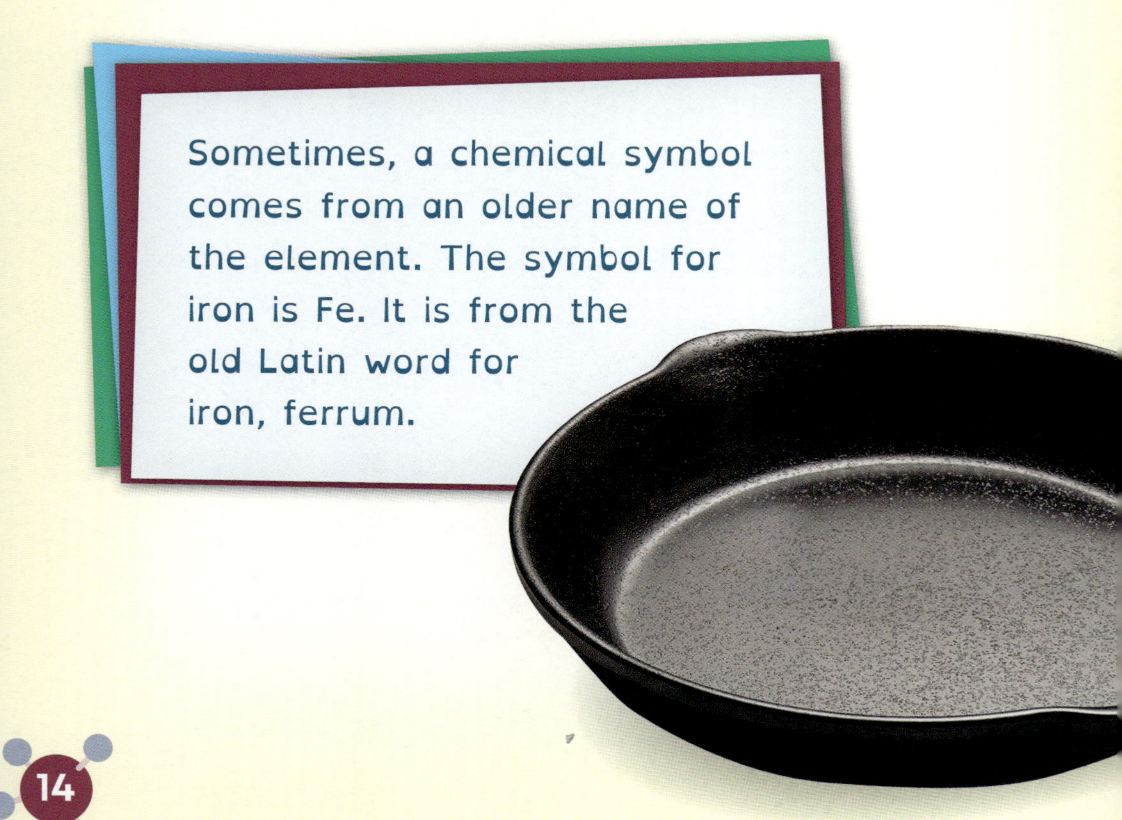

Sometimes, a chemical symbol comes from an older name of the element. The symbol for iron is Fe. It is from the old Latin word for iron, ferrum.

# Elements with Chemical Symbols from Old Names

| Element's current name | Element's original name | Chemical symbol |
|---|---|---|
| iron | ferrum | Fe |
| gold | aurum | Au |
| mercury | hydrargyrum | Hg |
| sodium | natrium | Na |
| lead | plumbum | Pb |

Pans are sometimes made from iron.

# Across and Down

The table organizes elements into seven rows. They are called periods. Periods are based on the number of electron shells. Elements in the first period have one electron shell per atom. The elements in the last row have seven.

There are two rows at the very bottom of the periodic table. They list elements from the sixth and seventh rows. Scientists break up these rows to make the table easier to read.

# The Periodic Table of Elements

This is the start of the first period.

Aluminum is in the third period.

| | | | | | | | | | | | | | | | | | |
|---|---|---|---|---|---|---|---|---|---|---|---|---|---|---|---|---|---|
| 1 H 1.008 Hydrogen | | | | | | | | | | | | | | | | | 2 He 4.002602 Helium |
| 3 Li 6.94 Lithium | 4 Be 9.0121831 Beryllium | | | | | | | | | | | 5 B 10.81 Boron | 6 C 12.011 Carbon | 7 N 14.007 Nitrogen | 8 O 15.999 Oxygen | 9 F 18.998403163 Fluorine | 10 Ne 20.1797 Neon |
| 11 Na 22.98976928 Sodium | 12 Mg 24.305 Magnesium | | | | | | | | | | | 13 Al 26.9815385 Aluminium | 14 Si 28.085 Silicon | 15 P 30.973761998 Phosphorus | 16 S 32.06 Sulfur | 17 Cl 35.45 Chlorine | 18 Ar 39.948 Argon |
| 19 K 39.0983 Potassium | 20 Ca 40.078 Calcium | 21 Sc 44.955908 Scandium | 22 Ti 47.867 Titanium | 23 V 50.9415 Vanadium | 24 Cr 51.9961 Chromium | 25 Mn 54.938044 Manganese | 26 Fe 55.845 Iron | 27 Co 58.933194 Cobalt | 28 Ni 58.6934 Nickel | 29 Cu 63.546 Copper | 30 Zn 65.38 Zinc | 31 Ga 69.723 Gallium | 32 Ge 72.630 Germanium | 33 As 74.921595 Arsenic | 34 Se 78.971 Selenium | 35 Br 79.904 Bromine | 36 Kr 83.798 Krypton |
| 37 Rb 85.4678 Rubidium | 38 Sr 87.62 Strontium | 39 Y 88.90584 Yttrium | 40 Zr 91.224 Zirconium | 41 Nb 92.90637 Niobium | 42 Mo 95.95 Molybdenum | 43 Tc 98 Technetium | 44 Ru 101.07 Ruthenium | 45 Rh 102.90550 Rhodium | 46 Pd 106.42 Palladium | 47 Ag 107.8682 Silver | 48 Cd 112.414 Cadmium | 49 In 114.818 Indium | 50 Sn 118.710 Tin | 51 Sb 121.760 Antimony | 52 Te 127.60 Tellurium | 53 I 126.90447 Iodine | 54 Xe 131.293 Xenon |
| 55 Cs 132.90545196 Caesium | 56 Ba 137.327 Barium | 57-71 | 72 Hf 178.49 Hafnium | 73 Ta 180.94788 Tantalum | 74 W 183.84 Tungsten | 75 Re 186.207 Rhenium | 76 Os 190.23 Osmium | 77 Ir 192.217 Iridium | 78 Pt 195.084 Platinum | 79 Au 196.966569 Gold | 80 Hg 200.592 Mercury | 81 Tl 204.38 Thallium | 82 Pb 207.2 Lead | 83 Bi 208.98040 Bismuth | 84 Po 209 Polonium | 85 At 210 Astatine | 86 Rn 222 Radon |
| 87 Fr 223 Francium | 88 Ra 226 Radium | 89-103 | 104 Rf 267 Rutherfordium | 105 Db 268 Dubnium | 106 Sg 269 Seaborgium | 107 Bh 270 Bohrium | 108 Hs 269 Hassium | 109 Mt 278 Meitnerium | 110 Ds 281 Darmstadtium | 111 Rg 281 Roentgenium | 112 Cn 285 Copernicium | 113 Nh 286 Nihonium | 114 Fl 289 Flerovium | 115 Mc 289 Moscovium | 116 Lv 293 Livermorium | 117 Ts 294 Tennessine | 118 Og 294 Oganesson |
| | | | 57 La 138.90547 Lanthanum | 58 Ce 140.116 Cerium | 59 Pr 140.90766 Praseodymium | 60 Nd 144.242 Neodymium | 61 Pm 145 Promethium | 62 Sm 150.36 Samarium | 63 Eu 151.964 Europium | 64 Gd 157.25 Gadolinium | 65 Tb 158.92535 Terbium | 66 Dy 162.500 Dysprosium | 67 Ho 164.93033 Holmium | 68 Er 167.259 Erbium | 69 Tm 168.93422 Thulium | 70 Yb 173.054 Ytterbium | 71 Lu 174.9668 Lutetium |
| | | | 89 Ac 227 Actinium | 90 Th 232.0377 Thorium | 91 Pa 231.03588 Protactinium | 92 U 238.02891 Uranium | 93 Np 237 Neptunium | 94 Pu 244 Plutonium | 95 Am 243 Americium | 96 Cm 247 Curium | 97 Bk 247 Berkelium | 98 Cf 251 Californium | 99 Es 252 Einsteinium | 100 Fm 257 Fermium | 101 Md 258 Mendelevium | 102 No 259 Nobelium | 103 Lr 266 Lawrencium |

These are part of the sixth and seventh periods.

Columns on the table are called groups or families. There are 18 groups. These element groups often have the same number of electrons in an atom's outer electron shell. Why is this important? These electrons play a big part in an element's chemical **properties**, or how it acts. Each element has unique properties.

An element's chemical properties are seen when it is part of a chemical reaction, such as when something catches on fire. Physical properties have to do with how an element looks.

# Most Common Elements

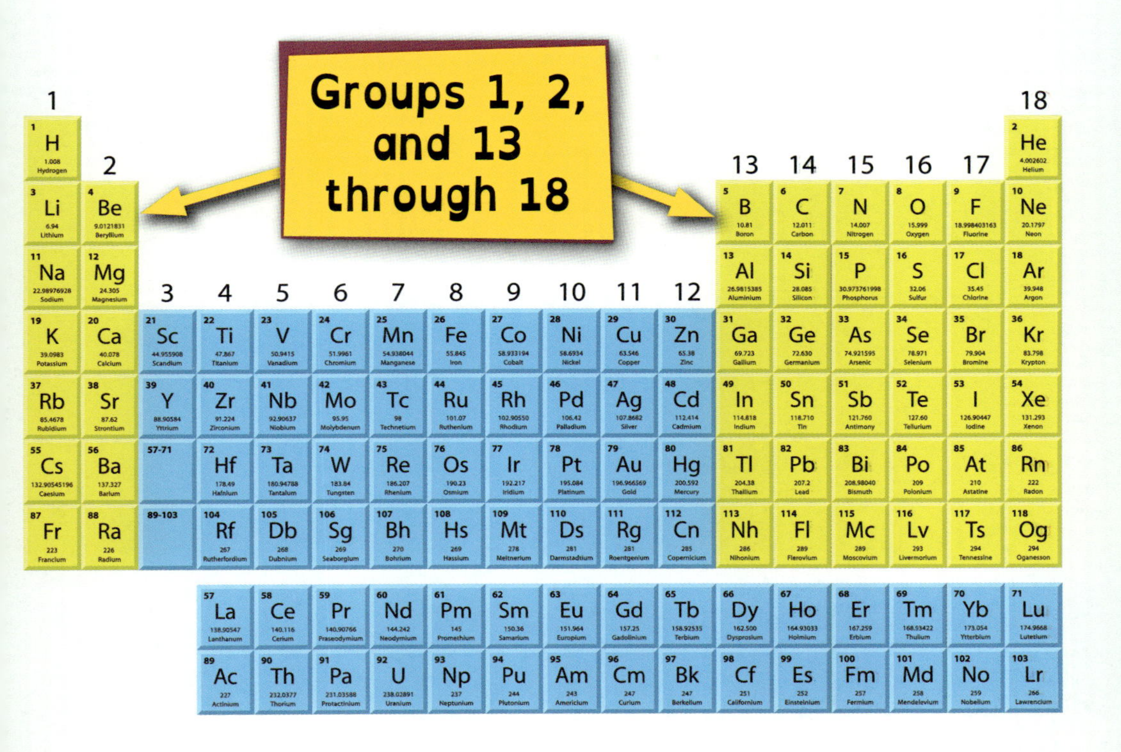


The groups on either end of the periodic table list the most common elements on Earth.

# Mostly Metal

Many of the elements on the periodic table are **metals**. Most metals look shiny. These elements share several other things in common. Heat and electricity move through these elements easily. They are good **conductors**. Metals are also often soft and can be shaped easily.

The properties of metals make them very useful. Copper is used to make the wires we find in many of our electronic devices. Aluminum is easily shaped into things like drinking cans.

# Metals on the Periodic Table

| 1 H 1.008 Hydrogen | | | | | | | | | | | | | | | | | 2 He 4.002602 Helium |
|---|---|---|---|---|---|---|---|---|---|---|---|---|---|---|---|---|---|
| 3 Li 6.94 Lithium | 4 Be 9.0121831 Beryllium | | | | | | | | | | | 5 B 10.81 Boron | 6 C 12.011 Carbon | 7 N 14.007 Nitrogen | 8 O 15.999 Oxygen | 9 F 18.998403163 Fluorine | 10 Ne 20.1797 Neon |
| 11 Na 22.98976928 Sodium | 12 Mg 24.305 Magnesium | | | | | | | | | | | 13 Al 26.9815385 Aluminium | 14 Si 28.085 Silicon | 15 P 30.973761998 Phosphorus | 16 S 32.06 Sulfur | 17 Cl 35.45 Chlorine | 18 Ar 39.948 Argon |
| 19 K 39.0983 Potassium | 20 Ca 40.078 Calcium | 21 Sc 44.955908 Scandium | 22 Ti 47.867 Titanium | 23 V 50.9415 Vanadium | 24 Cr 51.9961 Chromium | 25 Mn 54.938044 Manganese | 26 Fe 55.845 Iron | 27 Co 58.933194 Cobalt | 28 Ni 58.6934 Nickel | 29 Cu 63.546 Copper | 30 Zn 65.38 Zinc | 31 Ga 69.723 Gallium | 32 Ge 72.630 Germanium | 33 As 74.921595 Arsenic | 34 Se 78.971 Selenium | 35 Br 79.904 Bromine | 36 Kr 83.798 Krypton |
| 37 Rb 85.4678 Rubidium | 38 Sr 87.62 Strontium | 39 Y 88.90584 Yttrium | 40 Zr 91.224 Zirconium | 41 Nb 92.90637 Niobium | 42 Mo 95.95 Molybdenum | 43 Tc 98 Technetium | 44 Ru 101.07 Ruthenium | 45 Rh 102.90550 Rhodium | 46 Pd 106.42 Palladium | 47 Ag 107.8682 Silver | 48 Cd 112.414 Cadmium | 49 In 114.818 Indium | 50 Sn 118.710 Tin | 51 Sb 121.760 Antimony | 52 Te 127.60 Tellurium | 53 I 126.90447 Iodine | 54 Xe 131.293 Xenon |
| 55 Cs 132.90545196 Caesium | 56 Ba 137.327 Barium | 57-71 | 72 Hf 178.49 Hafnium | 73 Ta 180.94788 Tantalum | 74 W 183.84 Tungsten | 75 Re 186.207 Rhenium | 76 Os 190.23 Osmium | 77 Ir 192.217 Iridium | 78 Pt 195.084 Platinum | 79 Au 196.966569 Gold | 80 Hg 200.592 Mercury | 81 Tl 204.38 Thallium | 82 Pb 207.2 Lead | 83 Bi 208.98040 Bismuth | 84 Po 209 Polonium | 85 At 210 Astatine | 86 Rn 222 Radon |
| 87 Fr 223 Francium | 88 Ra 226 Radium | 89-103 | 104 Rf 267 Rutherfordium | 105 Db 268 Dubnium | 106 Sg 269 Seaborgium | 107 Bh 270 Bohrium | 108 Hs 269 Hassium | 109 Mt 278 Meitnerium | 110 Ds 281 Darmstadtium | 111 Rg 281 Roentgenium | 112 Cn 285 Copernicium | 113 Nh 286 Nihonium | 114 Fl 289 Flerovium | 115 Mc 289 Moscovium | 116 Lv 293 Livermorium | 117 Ts 294 Tennessine | 118 Og 294 Oganesson |
| | | | 57 La 138.90547 Lanthanum | 58 Ce 140.116 Cerium | 59 Pr 140.90766 Praseodymium | 60 Nd 144.242 Neodymium | 61 Pm 145 Promethium | 62 Sm 150.36 Samarium | 63 Eu 151.964 Europium | 64 Gd 157.25 Gadolinium | 65 Tb 158.92535 Terbium | 66 Dy 162.500 Dysprosium | 67 Ho 164.93033 Holmium | 68 Er 167.259 Erbium | 69 Tm 168.93422 Thulium | 70 Yb 173.054 Ytterbium | 71 Lu 174.9668 Lutetium |
| | | | 89 Ac 227 Actinium | 90 Th 232.0377 Thorium | 91 Pa 231.03588 Protactinium | 92 U 238.02891 Uranium | 93 Np 237 Neptunium | 94 Pu 244 Plutonium | 95 Am 243 Americium | 96 Cm 247 Curium | 97 Bk 247 Berkelium | 98 Cf 251 Californium | 99 Es 252 Einsteinium | 100 Fm 257 Fermium | 101 Md 258 Mendelevium | 102 No 259 Nobelium | 103 Lr 266 Lawrencium |

 Metals

Copper wire

# Nonmetals and Metalloids

The rest of the elements on the table are **nonmetals** or **metalloids** (MET-uhl-*oidz*). Nonmetals are not good conductors. They are not as strong as metals and break easily.

Metalloids have some properties of both metals and nonmetals. They usually look like metals but are not good conductors.

# Nonmetals and Metalloids on the Table

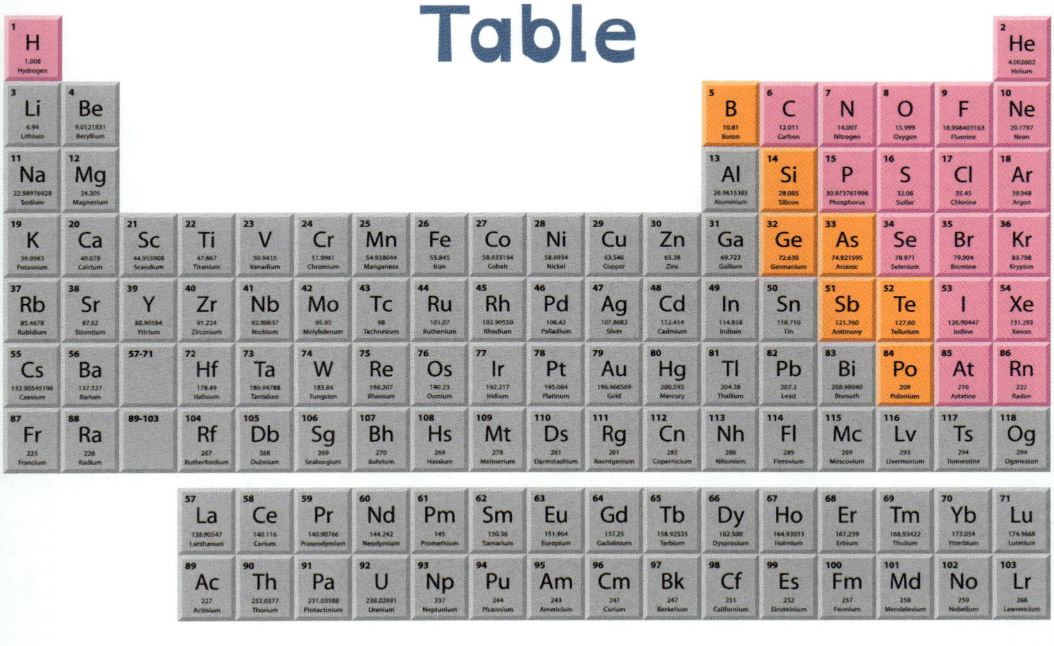


Nonmetals

Metalloids

The metalloid elements are found near one another on the table. They make up a line that separates metals and nonmetals.

**Boron is a metalloid.**

# Room for More

When the periodic table was first made, there were holes. Scientists worked to find the elements that would fill those holes. They used the table as their guide.

Scientists searched for elements with the right number of protons. The table gave clues about what properties the elements might have!

The first periodic table was made by Russian chemist Dmitri Mendeleev. He put it together before many elements were discovered. At the time, Mendeleev labeled only 66 elements.

Dmitri Mendeleev knew his table was missing some elements.

Scientists are still discovering new elements today. Some of these elements can be found in nature. Others are made in labs. There may even be new elements in space. Each new element will have its place on the periodic table.

Four new elements were added to the periodic table in 2016. Before they were found, they had temporary names. Their final names came from the places and people who made the discoveries.

Big machines help scientists look for new elements.

# Label the Table

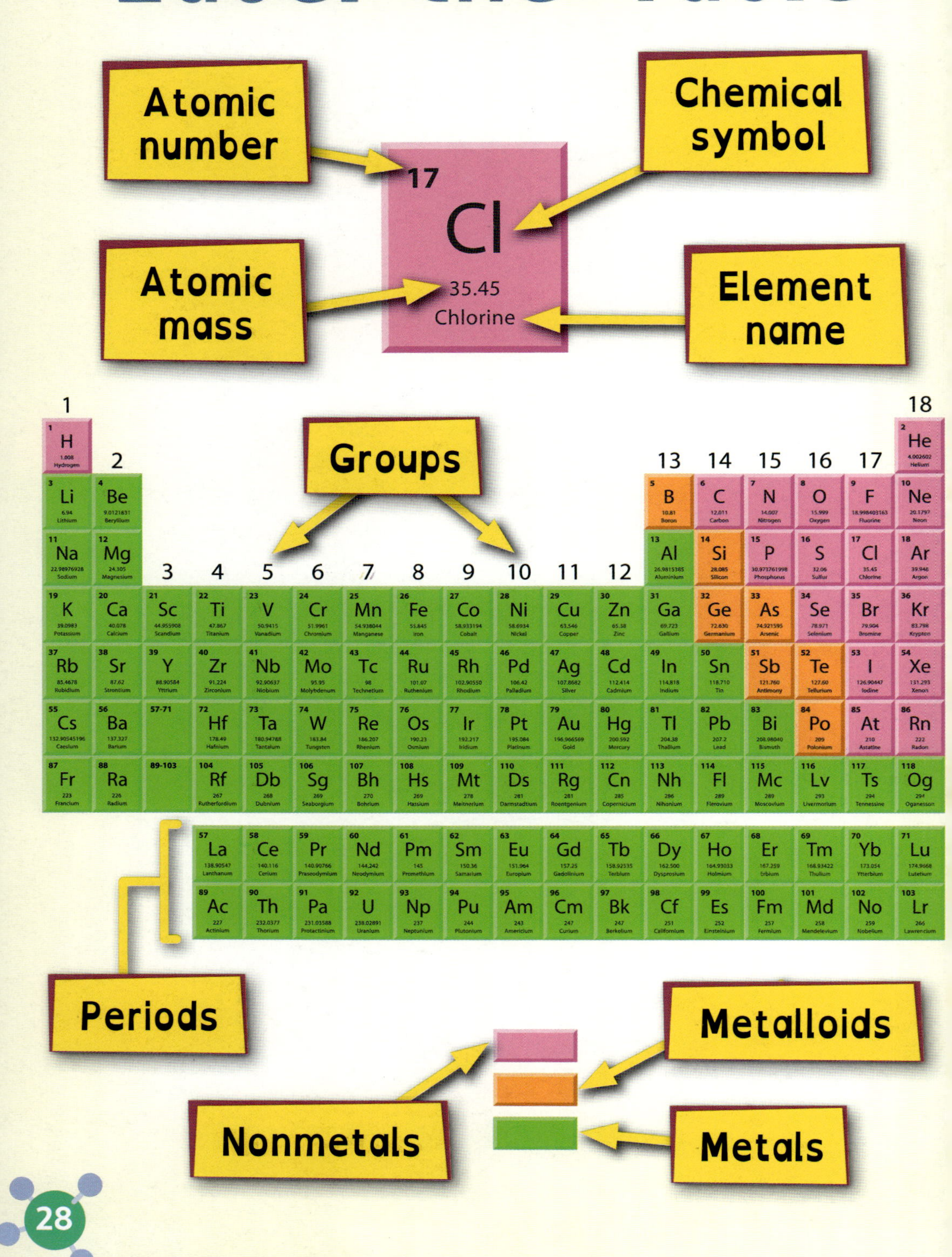

# SilverTips for SUCCESS

## ★ SilverTips for REVIEW

Review what you've learned. Use the text to help you.

### Define key terms

atomic number
atomic mass
chemical symbol
groups
periods

### Check for understanding

What can you find in each box of the periodic table?

How is the periodic table organized in rows? How is it organized in columns?

Describe the differences between metals, nonmetals, and metalloids.

### Think deeper

What can you predict about any elements scientists might discover in the future?

## SilverTips on TEST-TAKING

- **Make a study plan.** Ask your teacher what the test is going to cover. Then, set aside time to study a little bit every day.
- **Read all the questions carefully.** Be sure you know what is being asked.
- **Skip any questions** you don't know how to answer right away. Mark them and come back later if you have time.

# Glossary

**atoms** the tiny building blocks that make up every substance in the universe

**conductors** materials that heat or electricity can move through

**electrons** tiny parts of atoms that travel in shells around the nucleus

**elements** the things all around us that are made of one kind of atom

**metalloids** elements with properties of both metals and nonmetals

**metals** elements that are usually shiny, good conductors of heat and electricity, and can be easily shaped

**neutrons** tiny parts of an atom that can be found in the nucleus

**nonmetals** elements that do not have the properties of metals

**properties** the ways things look or act

**protons** tiny parts of an atom that can be found in the nucleus

# Read More

**Griffin, Mary.** *The Periodic Table (A Look at Chemistry)*. New York: Gareth Stevens, 2019.

**Rusick, Jessica.** *Inspecting Elements & the Periodic Table (Kid Chemistry Lab)*. Minneapolis: Abdo Publishing, 2022.

**Thomas, Isabel.** *Exploring the Elements: A Complete Guide to the Periodic Table*. New York: Phaidon Press, 2020.

# Learn More Online

1. Go to **www.factsurfer.com** or scan the QR code below.
2. Enter "**The Periodic Table**" into the search box.
3. Click on the cover of this book to see a list of websites.

# Index



# About the Author

Daniel R. Faust is a freelance writer of fiction and nonfiction. He lives in Brooklyn, NY.